1 MONTH OF FREE READING

at

www.ForgottenBooks.com

By purchasing this book you are eligible for one month membership to ForgottenBooks.com, giving you unlimited access to our entire collection of over 700,000 titles via our web site and mobile apps.

To claim your free month visit: www.forgottenbooks.com/free626768

ISBN 978-0-265-45181-6
PIBN 10626768

This book is a reproduction of an important historical work. Forgotten Books uses
state-of-the-art technology to digitally reconstruct the work, preserving the original format
whilst repairing imperfections present in the aged copy. In rare cases, an imperfection in
the original, such as a blemish or missing page, may be replicated in our edition. We do,
however, repair the vast majority of imperfections successfully; any imperfections that
remain are intentionally left to preserve the state of such historical works.

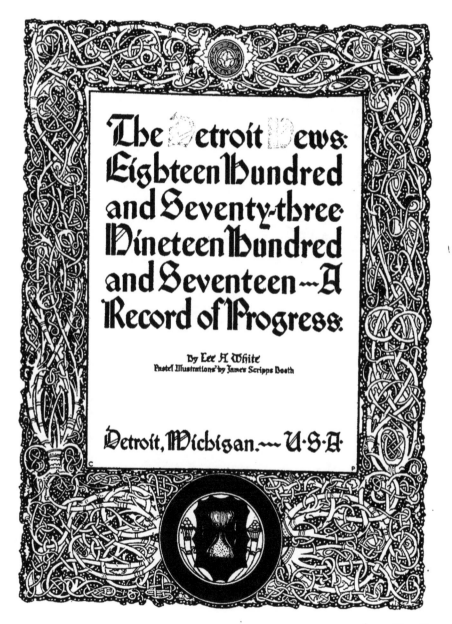

The Detroit News:
Eighteen Hundred and Seventy-three Nineteen Hundred and Seventeen—A Record of Progress.

By Lee A. White
Pastel Illustrations by James Scripps Booth

Detroit, Michigan.—U·S·A·

3 9

CONTENTS.

ILLUSTRATIONS.

THE DETROIT NEWS Building in 1917.

A CHRONICLE OF THE PAST.

HE picturesque bellman of Detroit, far back in 1781, had eight good shillings counted into his palm "for publishing to bring in straw" and fourteen "for drum-beating and publishing." Town Crier Williams probably gave thought to nothing more than the best means of spending his money, and the future's prospect of more. It is doubtful whether he dreamed of the coming of the newspaper that should make his vocation worse than precarious. Not even the seventh son of a seventh son would have been likely to forecast the construction of perhaps the most modern and distinctive newspaper establishment in the world within a stone's throw of the bellman's noisy path.

A generation passed before greater vision was manifested, and opportunity seized. The Rev. Fr. Gabriel Richard, whose figure in stone adorns a niche in the city hall of Detroit, very likely was averse to having notices nailed to the church door, as was the practice in the day of the Pontiac War, and he had a hand press brought overland from Baltimore which was ultimately used to print the first newspaper in Michigan.

Old St. Anne's Church, where Fr. Richard expounded the faith, was very much a center of news in the early nineteenth century; and since most of the population gathered there each Sunday, it was not unnatural that, with some show of clerical sanction, the doings of men should be cried under its eaves. Theophilus Mettez, a printer of religious books and subsequently a publisher of news, was wont to change his acolyte's garb for citizen's habit, after services, and, stationing himself outside the church, cry out the auction sales of merchandise, the races on the Rouge, and other events and entertainments to occur within the week. Thus did the "spoken newspaper" reach its highest point of development in this country.

Like the first newspaper in the United States, the first in Michigan apparently perished after a single issue had appeared. *The Michigan Essay* or *Impartial Observer*, as it was entitled, was to be a weekly, and it made its appearance August 31, 1809. It was a somewhat feeble attempt, even for the times, making no pretense at the publication of local items but confining itself to reprinting clippings from American papers four to six weeks old, and from English and Dutch papers printed as many months before, with a seasoning of poems, essays and letters to the editor. In deference to the French population, which predominated, a column and a half of the paper was printed in their language. The lone advertisement was of St. Anne's school. Possibly this had to do with the discouragement of the publisher, James M. Miller.

The Essay was most modest in size, due as much no doubt to the limitations of the press as to the scarcity of news. There were four pages, nine and a quarter by sixteen inches, each containing four columns of reading matter. Though a score of such newspapers could be lost within a present day edition of THE DETROIT NEWS, *The Essay* would compare rather favorably in size with THE NEWS at its birth, being approximately three-quarters as large.

The Detroit Gazette, Michigan's second paper, had better fortune. Apparently courage to attempt that at which *The Essay* had failed was not plentiful in the community, for *The Gazette's* appearance was as late as 1817; but it pursued a frequently troubled existence for thirteen years, ceasing publication April 22, 1830.

Forty-three years elapsed between the death of *The Gazette* and the birth of *The Evening News*, whose name became, on its thirty-second anniversary, August 23, 1905, THE DETROIT NEWS. Those forty-three years were disturbing to newspaper enterprise, it is certain, for Friend Palmer, in his reminiscences, published in 1884, recorded the rise and fall of one hundred and eighty-one newspapers and magazines in Detroit from the birth of *The Michigan Essay*.

At one stage in Detroit's life a somewhat distant neighbor seems to have taken pity upon it, but this was even before *The Essay*. *The Pittsburg Commonwealth*, issued far back in 1805 and published until 1809, paid special attention to news from Detroit; but very likely this was with a view to acquainting Pennsylvanians with the fortunes of relatives gone to the wilderness, and with opportunities for other pioneers.

THE DETROIT NEWS was founded by James Edmund Scripps, and appeared for the first time August 23, 1873. It was the first popular and low-priced daily newspaper in Michigan; and by the instant success of its radical departure from the conventions of newspaperdom, it became a voluble protest against inertia in journalism, and was heard countrywide. Thirty thousand dollars was the founder's working capital; but his chief investment was a vision of the future, and an eager intellect which had sought out the fundamental weaknesses of the old order, with which he had long been associated, if not identified.

Mr. Scripps was born in London, March 19, 1835, and came to this country when nine years old, settling near Rushville, Ill., with his parents. He entered newspaper work in 1857 as a reporter on *The Chicago Democratic Press*, afterward consolidated with *The Chicago Tribune*. At the age of twenty-four he came to Detroit as commercial editor of *The Detroit Daily Advertiser*, becoming part owner in 1861. Upon the consolidation of *The Advertiser* and *The Detroit Tribune*, in 1862, he became business manager, and a year later, editor.

His fourteen years of experience in Detroit furnished an excellent background of experience on which he based his conviction of a decade that a low priced evening newspaper would delight the city. The three morning papers had a total circulation of only 12,000 to 13,000, despite the fact that there were 20,000 families in Detroit. He felt sure that the public needed fresher news than they were getting, at a price within reason and at a time when it could be read.

Subsequently, as THE NEWS took on proportions past his dreams, Mr. Scripps was forced to modify some of his views; yet till his death he held to most of the articles of faith he set down in the leading editorial of the first issue. He believed the amount of money spent on the old "blanket sheets" was too great, and their circulation too small. He wished his paper to sell at a price that would insure "a wide diffusion of wholesome literature." He hoped to be able to keep advertising rates low enough to appeal to the hitherto discouraged advertiser, and he meant to teach the business man that wisely prepared copy, frequently changed, would insure adequate returns from his investment. He felt sure that the average citizen was given more than he could read in his scant leisure, and that not only was brevity desirable but the selection of material should be such as to insure the widest possible interest. He was free to put behind him any convention of journalism that would not survive the test of public interest; and he meant to emphasize fact, not opinion, letting the readers of his paper reach, unhampered, their own clear convictions, for which reason he spurned partisan support and set sail in the clear sea of independence. He had not had an opportunity to realize these aims in his previous associations, and he bent himself enthusiastically to his purposes when THE NEWS was born.

The little publication of 1873 is quite dwarfed beside the 36-page daily editions common in 1918; it may have seemed relatively insignificant compared with the "blanket sheets" of its own day. It was a four-page publication measuring less than twenty inches in length and a little over thirteen in width —a trifle more than half the size of a page of THE NEWS today. In typography it was hardly distinguished; in that day the art of "dressing" a paper was young, and little or no thought was given to anything but legibility. Advertisements, as was common in that generation, occupied half of the front page—three of the six columns. But there was a salt-air freshness in the style in which the items were written (few stories exceeded a paragraph in length), and this, in contrast with the stilted diction and dull content of the average newspaper of the seventies, was not without its influence in determining the immediate success of THE NEWS.

In retrospect, some years afterward, Mr. Scripps described the change in news writing, especially with reference to personal items, which lost the conventional fulsomeness and became, instead, geniality itself. "With no political ends to serve and with entire absence of ill-feeling," he wrote, "the city editor began to handle the city's news with much of the same freedom that would be allowed in conversation. It was a revelation to staid, prosy Detroit, and THE NEWS quickly got the reputation of being a 'sensational' sheet, although compared with later up-to-date journals in our larger cities it was commendably moderate and respectable. Naturally some took offense at it, but the people generally liked it, even the so-called better class."

He knew, and often said, that had he endeavored to compete with the old papers on their own ground, he would have sunk speedily such capital as he had and was able to command. But by producing a sprightly paper, which still set principle above popularity and was constitutionally optimistic, he commanded approving attention. The several thousand dollars that he lost the first year was soon won back, the second year netting him $6,000.

The popularity of the paper was never in question. No paper in Detroit had ever printed on the day of its first appearance as many copies as THE NEWS; and in the fourth issue the publisher announced that the average circulation to date

The Evening News.

The First Issue, August 23, 1873,

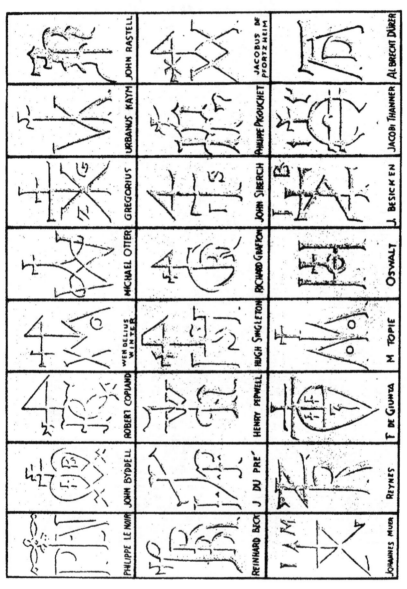

Devices of Master Printers of Another Age Adorn the Exterior.

was between eight and nine thousand—from four to six times the city distribution of any contemporary. Its dominance throughout its history has never been denied. Mr. Scripps had dreamed of a circulation of 10,000. In ten years he had to serve 40,000 subscribers. In the last year of his life, 1906, the circulation was in excess of 100,000; and now, twelve years later, is more than 225,000. In its first year The News sold one copy for every fourteen residents of Detroit; today the ratio is approximately one to four and a half.

Necessarily, such growth entailed constant alterations in the housing of The News, and frequent additions to the mechanical equipment. From its temporary site on Griswold Street, The News had moved to Shelby Street, between Congress and Larned, two months after the first issue went on the streets. It occupied that land until October 15, 1917—forty-four years—but the successive additions of parcels of ground, and the continual construction of new units to allow for the expansion of the paper, erased from the memories of all but a few the humble origin of The News.

The first home had been a simple frame house, set well forward to the sidewalk, and at the corner of an alley. To this was added a little one-story brick press room which served until 1877, when a more commodious and appropriate building, 60 by 30 feet, was erected.

Ultimately The News occupied a four-floored building fronting 120 feet on Shelby Street and 140 feet on Larned; a building that was never free from the altering hands of carpenters and masons, who struggled vainly to meet the increasing demands of a growing newspaper. The early years of Mr. Scripps' career as publisher of The News were years of desperate effort. He was constantly straining for funds with which to increase ground area or floor space or printing and publishing equipment; and family and friends were required to show their faith in both his vision and enterprise. Each stone, each brick, each timber in the building, up to the year 1888, represented the founder's relish for labor and devotion to the institution he had built.

Mr. Scripps founded The News in the year of that financial crisis of dreadful memory—the "panic of '73"—but perhaps this augured well. He could not look forward to more desperate times; and he was immediately given opportunity to demonstrate how much sounder were his business principles than those of his contemporaries.

The times in which the paper was born and the character of the events with which the editorial department had to deal are glimpsed among the more or less romantic pages of history.

Detroit was a gas-lighted town of a hundred thousand population in 1873. Five years were to pass before arc lights were to be devised in the neighboring city of Cleveland; six years before Edison was to demonstrate his efficient incandescent bulb at Menlo Park; three years before Bell was to take out his patents on the telephone. Horse cars had been in use less than a decade in the city; electric street railways were not to occupy the thoroughfares of Detroit for nineteen years.

The early issues of THE NEWS gave more attention to the Carlist insurrection in Spain than any other foreign intelligence; and that futile campaign in behalf of the pretender to the throne was a staple of news for nearly three years.

Immigration was at once a matter of pride and concern to the nation at large; and the year THE NEWS was founded 459,803 persons found their way to the hospitable shores of the country—the largest number in a single year before 1881. Reconstruction problems and Ku Klux Klan activities in the South filled the fretful telegraph wires. The purchase of Alaska was still referred to with disgust as a wasteful expenditure; the lapse of six years had not downed the contemptuous references in the press to the folly of paying $7,200,000 for "Seward's icebox," now so richly prized. But the failure of Jay Cooke & Co. in Philadelphia, precipitating the panic, was the biggest domestic news.

Naturally, and wisely, THE NEWS emphasized local news, almost to the exclusion of all other save that of the outlying districts of the state wherein the publisher expected it to have a somewhat extensive circulation. In the fourth issue it was remarked with editorial pride that *"The Evening News,* this afternoon, contains about seventy items of important city news, besides three extended articles on subjects not touched by the morning papers. All the other papers of Detroit have succeeded in gathering about thirty facts."

Among these items are found proud reference to the fact that the city had thirty-one mail carriers and four postal clerks, and that the inhabitants wrote 12,000 letters a day; that there were 9,358 men in Detroit capable of bearing arms (a reference to the need of men in the army, for Custer was then engaged in his Yellowstone expedition against unruly Indians); that a "live English Duke" had passed by the city; that the city's bank balance approached a quarter of a million dollars, and that Mayor Schultz planned to open a free chess room near the waterfront on Bates Street.

It took Mr. Scripps a very little while to find tangible evidence of the revolution he was working in local newspaper circles, and the first of the contemporaries of THE NEWS to acknowledge its dominance and yield position was *The Detroit Daily Union*, a publication started by journeyman printers after a strike in 1865. It was rarely successful for such a newspaper, and persisted for nine years, discontinuing in 1874, THE NEWS absorbing its circulation.

Newspaper publishers and men who had an itch for distinction in journalism were quick to sense the virtue of the business and editorial methods of THE NEWS. In the counting room a cash basis prevailed for advertiser and subscriber alike, and each evening Mr. Scripps knew to a penny the status of his financial affairs. In the editorial room new American standards of geniality, brevity and pungency in newspaper writing were being set. Many a publisher from more or less distant cities came to Detroit to learn what he could of the radical departures and striking successes of the youthful enterprise.

THE NEWS not alone inspired but fathered important publishing ventures. In November, 1878, its first offspring, *The Cleveland Press*, was established; in 1880 *The Chronicle* began publication in St. Louis, Mo., and in 1881 *The Cincinnati Post* was added to the group. Out of this league of newspapers ultimately grew a powerful organization with extensive holdings, but James Edmund Scripps decided that there was abundant occupation for his talent and energy in Detroit, and he withdrew from active part in the management of all papers excepting THE DETROIT NEWS, at a later date even disposing of his interest in the papers which he had helped found.

By 1890 Mr. Scripps had sensed the material advantages that would accrue to the newspaper which should lower its price in the local field to one cent, but he was disposed to experiment before changing the policy of THE NEWS. He started the independent Times Publishing Company in August of that year, and published for two years *The Detroit Times*. The paper sold at a penny and convinced the founder of the correctness of his surmise. *The Times* was suspended and its circulation lists were taken over by THE NEWS, whose price was reduced shortly afterward.

Contemporary with THE NEWS was a morning paper whose honorable history is not yet forgotten, though it exists now only as a bit of blood in the veins of THE NEWS. It appeared as *The Detroit Tribune* for the first time October 23, 1849, and was a weekly Whig newspaper. A month after it was established a daily morning edition was begun, and in June of 1851 it entered the evening field temporarily. Its history is one of many consolidations, and the papers which figured date back to the *Northwestern Journal.* This publication, founded in 1829, subsequently became *The Detroit Journal and Michigan Advertiser,* still later *The Detroit Journal and Courier,* and appeared as a daily in 1836 under the title *The Detroit Daily Advertiser.* It was merged with *The Democrat and Enquirer* in 1855, and with *The Detroit Daily Tribune* in 1862, when it acquired the new name, *The Advertiser and Tribune.* In 1877 *The Advertiser and Tribune* was consolidated with *The Detroit Daily Post,* which Zachariah Chandler had fostered by way of punishment of the old Republican *Tribune,* which was showing signs of disturbing independence of the senator. The name of the united papers was *The Post and Tribune,* and its editor was the distinguished Gen. Carl Schurz. In 1884 the unwieldy name was shortened to *The Post,* and a year later the property was sold to Minneapolis men who organized The Detroit Tribune Printing Co. and rechristened the publication *The Detroit Tribune.* Two further transfers brought *The Tribune* into the hands of Mr. Scripps, January 1, 1891, and its ownership was unchanged from then till the merger with THE DETROIT NEWS, February 1, 1915.

THE NEWS brought forth a Sunday edition November 30, 1884, which was amalgamated with *The Sunday Tribune,* October 15, 1893, and entitled *The Sunday News-Tribune.* This compounded name persisted during a brief period when the daily *Tribune* had lost its identity and was a morning edition of THE NEWS; it was still used after *The Tribune* ceased to appear. But the day before THE NEWS entered its new home, exactly twenty-four years from the date of consolidation of the two Sunday papers, the publishers revived the old name of THE DETROIT SUNDAY NEWS.

The one venture of THE NEWS outside the field of daily newspapers was not a notable success. For a period of about five years, from 1887 to 1892, a weekly edition, *The Echo,* was published. It consisted largely of matter reprinted directly from THE NEWS, in somewhat condensed form, and was intended to summarize the week's happenings.

Domination of the local field was the constant aim of THE NEWS, but it did not fail to win approbation in far lands, even in its youth. In 1888 R. Raleigh,

·Craftsmanship of Unusual Excellence Has Enriched the Main Lobby.

The Second Floor Lobby Opens upon All Public Offices.

editor of the Sidney, Australia, *News*, wrote in his paper of his tour of America and his investigation of publishing enterprises. The editorial page of THE DETROIT NEWS he gave high rank because of its able and spirited treatment of general subjects, and, said he, "It struck me as the best evening newspaper I saw in the whole country." He perceived that a new note had been sounded in American journalism.

Ten years later THE NEWS was proving consistent in its enterprise by sending a special correspondent with each of the five Michigan regiments that reached the front during the Spanish-American war; thirty years later the readers of THE DETROIT NEWS were still being offered unequaled dispatches in a national crisis that necessitated the tapping of new and old lines of communication to the uttermost parts of the earth. It has persistently met every obligation that the eagerness of the public suggested, and has even more often anticipated public interest in great events and small.

In acknowledging this responsibility from the very beginning, the founder, who in 1888 retired from the active management of the paper, recognized the necessity of keeping pace in facilities for newspaper production. He died May 29, 1906, with his dearest dream unrealized—the construction of an appropriate building for the greater DETROIT NEWS.

An Ideal Expressed in Architecture.

THE new home of THE DETROIT NEWS was not conceived in a moment, then hastened to realization. It represents a quarter of a century's accumulation of plans made and abandoned under pressure of unexpected progress, of financial depressions, of advancing ideals, of invention and the resultant change in necessary equipment and housing of a great newspaper.

George G. Booth, now president of The Evening News Association, was called to the assistance of Mr. Scripps in 1888, when the founder's health had been undermined by the incessant demands made upon his time and energy. Before he had been with THE NEWS two years, Mr. Booth, foreseeing the inevitable development of the institution and the consequent need for more commodious quarters, laid plans for a new building on the old Shelby Street site. By the time THE NEWS was ready to proceed with the task, the needs of the publication and the prospects for the future convinced the publishers that the location was inappropriate.

Property at the southeast corner of Shelby Street and Lafayette Boulevard was purchased, and the proprietors of THE NEWS went so far as to choose an architect and make personal inspection of leading newspaper buildings throughout the country, with a view to the appropriation of acceptable ideas and the prevention of mistakes made by others. A delay of a year ensued, during which time the plans were perfected and published. Then, and then only, THE NEWS considered erecting a structure which should be both an office building and a publishing plant, elaborate in appointments and pretentious in size. It was designed to serve the public in a variety of ways, and a vast and luxurious section of the building was reserved to accommodate the Board of Commerce of that time.

A financial disturbance prevented the materialization of this idea. When calm was restored, this site was, in its turn, discarded as being inadequate. Henceforth Mr. Booth's conviction that the primary purpose of a newspaper's home must never be subordinated to any alien purpose prevailed. He was convinced, as a result of his experience in erecting the justly praised *Grand Rapids Press* building, that no interest, large or small, should be permitted to intrude;

24

that the institutional character of the newspaper ought not to be obscured; that the designing of a building to serve two purposes must result in the sacrifice of one.

Then, for the fourth time, the publishers found themselves forced to undertake extensive alterations and enlargements of the old plant, amounting almost to reconstruction. Search was immediately begun for ground which would, without fail, meet the demands put upon it for years to come, whatever the strides of Detroit and The News might be. And the property extending 280 feet on Second Avenue, from Fort Street to Lafayette Boulevard, with a frontage of 150 feet on these two highways, was obtained at a cost of nearly a quarter of a million dollars.

It was a coincidence that The News chose for its building site the old homestead of Zachariah Chandler, who, in the day of his political puissance, had chastised *The Tribune* by capitalizing a rival sheet.

It was deemed necessary to make The News, as a public institution, reasonably accessible to the people, convenient to the sources of supplies, and within the smallest circle that would encompass the gates to rail and water carriers. Much of the ordinary business of the public with the newspaper is now transacted through downtown offices, numerous sub-stations throughout the city, and over the telephone; but the building is easily reached by foot, by Fort Street car line or by automobile, from Campus Martius. It lies in an area of comparative quiet that, while perhaps not necessary to good journalism, is nevertheless appreciated by the staff.

In the two years intervening between the purchase of this property in November, 1913, and the breaking of ground in November, 1915, all the quarter century's careful study of the subject was applied to the development of the plans for the building. And in these, as in preceding days, the old Shelby Street quarters were constantly being overhauled, refurbished, remodeled, in an endeavor to keep the long outgrown plant equal to the tremendous strain put upon it by the progress of both the city and The News.

Every impulse to exclude or include an idea, in the development of the plans, was tested with a single consideration—the requirements of the newspaper. The faith of the publishers in the city, in the business integrity of the area served by The News, in the publication itself, made a vision of the future's demands upon the structure naturally broad. Yet while the building must needs be subject to expansion, it was imperative that limits be set which would make utility certain. Its five floors have a usable area of 144,484 square feet, fully occupied, and the content is 2,673,000 cubic feet. That the building should be, so far as can be learned, the largest exclusive newspaper plant in the world, was not an ambition; it was purely incidental to the satisfying of specific needs.

For the first time, a serious and successful attempt was made to apply modern factory efficiency principles to the organization of a great newspaper; and this was true equally of the building and the equipment. Yet it was not necessary to sacrifice good taste in any instance.

The publishers of THE NEWS view the newspaper as a semi-public institution, holding a tacit franchise from the people, and under obligation to supply the reader with a truthful account of things happening, as well as interpretations of more complex events. Mr. Booth, to whom fell the task of supervising the design, construction and equipment of the building, was determined that the new home of THE NEWS should possess the dignity of style, chastity of spirit and substantiality appropriate to an institution which is aware of its intimate association with the welfare of the individual and the state. The achievement of this end was made possible through the services of Albert Kahn, whose high qualifications as an architect insured a structure of superior design; whose willingness and ability to enter into the spirit of the publishers made it inevitable that the building should satisfy completely the industrial needs of its occupants.

Escape was sought from the classic and Renaissance traditions which have too often been but indifferently appropriate to modern needs, and by daring adaptation of medieval precedents a building that acknowledges its European prototype, and yet is really and essentially American, was realized.

Nothing seemed so in harmony with the character, the purposes and the ideals of the newspaper, in the way of building materials, as stone; and this was chosen. The result has been a pleasing relief from the monotonous array of terra cotta and brick and plate glass which afflicts the eye in the business district of any modern American city.

The structural expression is a notable feature of the design. No endeavor was made to conceal the presence of a concrete frame, which is easily identified in the series of piers and spandrels. Indeed, emphasis was lent to the piers by their extension in unbroken line and bold relief, from pavement to parapet's top; and between the piers, mullions of stone, whose bases merge into the arch ring above the generous first story windows, pass through the second and third

The President's Suite Is on the Mezzanine Floor.

The Vice-President's Office is the Connecting Link between Editorial and Business Departments.

stories to the parapet. The fine and unusual vertical effect obtained by this treatment is further augmented by the dominant and thoroughly masculine pylons at
the corners of the building. Their broad surfaces of stone are unadorned, broken
only by single windows, and surmounted by pyramidal tops. The architect was
signally successful in gaining an effect of massiveness and solidity without sacrific-
ing the light so utterly necessary to the occupants.

The decorative phases of the exterior are three in number. The broad parapet of stone which encircles the roof bears, on the Fort Street and Lafayette
Boulevard facades, inscriptions in raised stone letters of singularly attractive form.
In tribute to the fathers of the printing craft, the fluted stone spandrels below the
third story windows carry carved ornaments, heraldic shields and in some cases
simple square blocks on all of which are graven the colophons, or printers' marks,
of the storied past. They were the devices or initials of master craftsmen by
which their works were identified. Among those represented are Albrecht Durer,
incomparable artist in several fields; Richard Grafton, who was heavily fined and
committed to old Fleet Street prison because he printed bibles for the common
folk without let of king or clergy; rash Hugh Singleton, whose printing of an
indiscreet reflection upon Queen Elizabeth's amours cost him his liberty, and two
of his associates their good right hands; and a representative of the Aldus family,
from whom was derived the name of the "Aldine Prints." By making these
symbols the chief and characteristic decoration of the exterior of the building,
The News confesses to the world its obligation to those who laid the foundation
of learning and liberal education in "the art preservative of all the arts." And in
consonance with this decorative feature are the carved stone figures at the heads
of four piers on the Lafayette facade representing distinguished pioneers in printing: Johannes Gutenberg, to whom is popularly attributed the invention of the
art of printing from movable types; Christophe Plantin, a French bookbinder,
printer and publisher, from whose office in Antwerp were issued some of the
most accurate and beautifully embellished works of the Sixteenth Century;
William Caxton, the first English printer; and Benjamin Franklin, the most distinguished and successful of America's early printers and editors.

Supplementing these fitting touches are elaborately carved arch mouldings, and
the richly ornamented iron work of the first floor windows and exterior lighting
fixtures, the latter designed to flood the building with a warm glow of light at night.

The spirit of restraint which saved the exterior of the building from anything
resembling over elaboration also guided architect and decorator in the treatment
of the interior.

Entering, one passes through a wrought steel vestibule of exquisite design and simple dignity into a spacious and high vaulted lobby wherein the stone of the exterior is used again in the walls.   Indeed, the same structural and decorative scheme extends up the broad stairway to the second floor lobby from which the public has access to all the departments with which it has business.   The main lobby has the cathedral quality of winning greater devotion the longer one abides; and a pure delight is born of contemplating the refined Renaissance coloring and modeling in the ceiling, the symbolic lunettes, and the steel grilles in the tympanums at either end.   The metal work in the lobby is of the highest decorative importance, and in craftsmanship is comparable to fine achievements of the middle ages.

The decorator sought to use his art so the ceiling might become, not a picture apart, but an integral part of the lobby; and to this end he was rather severe in the reduction of colors and design.   The ensemble is grayish, though the means to this end were reds, oranges, greens, blues, violets and gold leaf treated in Etruscan finish.   The endeavor to lend to the soffits and lunettes the Florentine spirit in color, plus the patina that has come with the ages, was highly successful; and there is promise of increasingly pleasing qualities as time mellows the pigments.   The same tone and quality were carried into the second floor lobby by the running of borders and lines of stony texture in gold and colors.

A delightful phase of the decoration is an illuminated globe of iridescent glass, a reproduction of a medieval concept of the world, with its quaint distortions of continents and its mysterious seas dotted with galleons, serpents of awful mien, and whales of strange habits and habitats.

The editorial rooms and business offices on the second floor have been treated with the clear intention of recalling the simplicity of the building from without. Between the sweepingly broad oak wainscoting and the flat coffered ceilings a neutral tint has been imposed upon the walls by a medieval process of stippling in five colors.

Justifiable departure from the general severity of the building is found in two suites of private offices.   On the mezzanine floor are the offices of the president, purposely set apart from the rest of the organization, so that he may exclude himself from interference with the well-working business mechanism of the plant, and yet, at will, take a hand in the affairs of any department.   In the corridor just outside these offices are hung attractive pastel pictures of familiar scenes in the old building, done by James Scripps Booth, a grandson of the founder. On the second floor, at the junction of the editorial and business departments, are the offices of William E. Scripps, son of the founder of The Detroit News, vice-president; Hereward S. Scott, general manager, and George E. Miller, editor. These rooms are in a modified Elizabethan style, provided with delicately modeled ceilings, and elaborately wainscoted in oak on which the woodcarver has exercised his fine and ancient art. These suites have all essential intimacy, and were designed as a foil to the general simplicity of the building. Leaded glass casement windows have given them a gracious individuality, and a spirit of detachment from the brash outer world.

Another generation of critics, less intimately interested in the development of the building and blessed therefore with a better perspective, must say of what significance it is architecturally; whether it is, in fact, as has been said, "a point from which to reckon." But it is a building of wholesome conception in design; well proportioned and impressive in its magnitude; efficient in construction; admirably adapted to its purpose. It seems, in truth, to convey to the onlooker a consciousness of the high import of journalism; a sense of the security of a democratic state whose most effective voice is in a press gifted with vision for the future and possessed of a proper respect for its responsibilities.

High on parapet, where the eyes of all may see, are chiseled the declared functions and high purposes of the press. The inscriptions, of which Professor F. N. Scott, of the University of Michigan, is the author, are, in the words of the president of the The News, "a reminder of service rendered and those ideals we are pledged to attain":

Mirror of the public mind · · Interpreter of the public intent
Troubler of the public conscience

Reflector of every human interest · · Friend of every righteous cause
Encourager of every generous act

Bearer of intelligence · · Dispeller of ignorance and prejudice
A light shining into all dark places

Promoter of civic welfare and civic pride · · Bond of civic unity
Protector of civic rights

The Detroit News.

Scourge of evil doers · · Exposer of secret iniquities
Unrelenting foe of privilege and corruption

Voice of the lowly and oppressed · · Advocate of the friendless
Righter of public and private wrongs

Chronicler of facts · · Sifter of rumors and opinions
Minister of the truth that makes men free

Reporter of the new · · Remembrancer of the old and tried
Herald of what is to come

Defender of civil liberty · · Strengthener of loyalty
Pillar and stay of democratic government

Upbuilder of the home · · Nourisher of the community spirit
Art, letters, and science of the common people

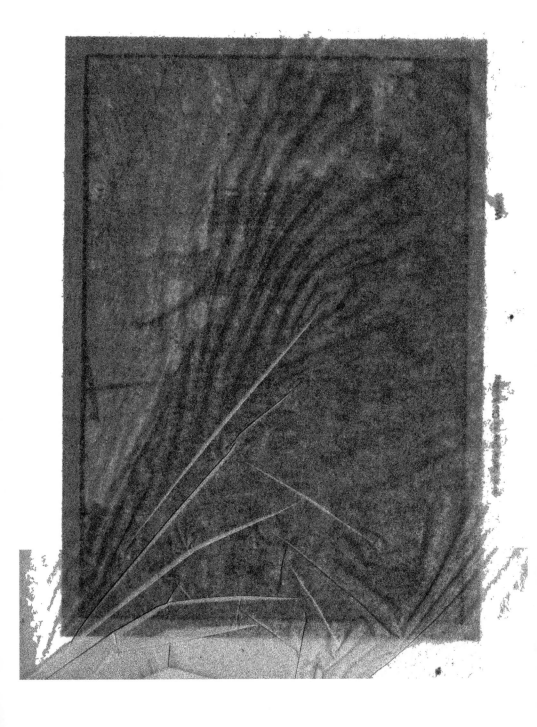

THE DETROIT NEWS

SCOURGE OF EVIL-DOERS   EXPOSER OF SECRET INIQUITIES
UNRELENTING FOE OF PRIVILEGE AND CORRUPTION

VOICE OF THE LOWLY AND OPPRESSED   ADVOCATE OF
RIGHTER OF PUBLIC AND PRIVATE WRONGS

CHRONICLER OF FACTS   SIFTER OF RUMORS AND
MINISTER OF THE TRUTH THAT MAKES MEN FREE

PROMOTER OF THE NEW   REMEMBRANCER OF THE OLD AND TRIED
HERALD OF WHAT MAY COME

DEFENDER OF CIVIL LIBERTY   STRENGTHENER OF LOYALTY
PILLAR AND STAY OF DEMOCRATIC GOVERNMENT

UPBUILDER OF THE HOME   NOURISHER OF THE COMMUNITY
CRITERIA AND STRENGTH OF THE COMMON PEOPLE

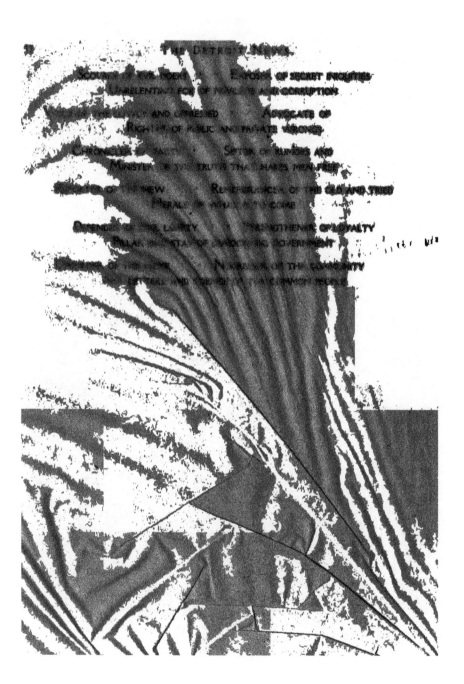

In an Earlier Day the Old Building Was Itself a Showplace of the Newspaper World.

HEALTH, COMFORT AND RECREATION.

THE personal equation, in a newspaper plant, is a particularly important one. It is only through the development of a spirit which transcends the individual that a newspaper may have an enduring personality. Each must give himself to the institution in order that its life may be renewed— which necessitates that every member of the staff develop to the utmost his particular talents, and surrender these to the common end: the production of a newspaper of individuality. Material agencies in the development of this spirit of self-abnegation are unnecessary; it is too characteristic of the types who enter newspaper work to need artificial culture. Employes of THE DETROIT NEWS were as loyal, as devoted to their calling, as willing to submerge themselves for the good of the institution in the old frame house where the paper was born as in the notable structure they now occupy. It was felt that, in the new building, every possible consideration should be shown the employes, every attention paid to their comfort and convenience, not as a purchase price of effort but as their right.

Recreational advantages are conspicuous, and chief of these is the conference room, located on the second floor adjacent to the restaurant. It is capacious, measuring thirty-two by fifty-seven feet, and is richly and most comfortably furnished—a clubby sort of room, where the chimed hours of midday are sped with music, good reading and the colorful and stimulating conversation common to newspaperdom. Here, too, are held departmental and inter-departmental staff conferences, where policy and action are outlined; here appear, occasionally, distinguished journalists and men of affairs to address the editorial staff; here, in holiday spirit, dances have been held. Chamber music recitals, formal receptions and festivities are within the scope of the room; and on the occasion of the visits of distinguished foreign editors to Detroit as guests of the United States, it was the scene of luncheons in their honor. Moving picture and stereopticon equipment adds to the availability of the room for purposes of education and entertainment, and THE NEWS contemplates extending the facilities of the room, when the occasion is sufficient, to public-spirited citizens engaged in beneficent enterprises. The Young Writers' Club, fostered by the juvenile section of THE DETROIT SUNDAY NEWS, finds it an excellent meeting place. Portable rostrums and chairs for three hundred and fifty are stored close at hand.

The tiled portion of the roof is utilized by the athletically inclined as a tennis court, and the high parapet of the building acts as an effective backstop. The pyramidal-roofed towers, which are an architectural feature of the corners of the building, offer excellent handball courts in winter.

On the ground floor of the building, at the corner of Lafayette Boulevard and Second Avenue, is a newsboys' salesroom of generous dimensions where the youngsters who handle papers in the neighboring down-town districts gather to buy the various editions. Gymnasium mats and boxing gloves make possible many a strenuous but amicable bout, usually refereed by indulgent police officers or employes. A great playroom, suitable for the use of several hundred boys, was constructed in the basement below the salesroom, but due to changing administration of street sales comparatively few newsboys come to the building for their papers. Time was when THE NEWS, a pioneer in such welfare work for news-boys, maintained an auditorium, swimming pool and other club facilities for the youngsters, and even organized and provided a director for a newsboys' band that was famous in its day.

Effort in an afternoon newspaper plant reaches its peak around midday, and employes are for the most part compelled to lunch hurriedly. THE NEWS has provided them with an excellent restaurant, operated on the serve-self plan, where food is furnished at low cost. A low paneling divides the restaurant into two parts, one for office employes and one for mechanics, a convenience that permits the latter to enjoy the advantages of the cafe without changing their clothes. The kitchen is a model of compactness, and is furnished with all manner of ingenious devices to facilitate the work of the chefs and insure sanitary conditions. All food is subjected to daily inspection by the staff dietitian and nurse.

Industrial accidents in the newspaper world are not particularly numerous, nor are the injuries suffered by employes often of a serious nature. In a plant employing five hundred workmen a liberal allowance for a first aid hospital was necessary, however.

Because of the large amount of heavily geared machinery, notably the presses, there are from time to time painful if not serious lacerations and crushed fingers and hands. The stereotyping process, involving the handling of many tons of molten metal daily, is not without its tragic incidents, usually more or less superficial burns. The shipping department, with its forty-one trucks engaged in the delivery of the paper, is sometimes the scene of accidents resulting in fractures, or, more often, sprains, contusions and lacerations of sufficient consequence to warrant special attention. Added to these are the emergencies inevitable where so many labor: fainting spells, hemorrhages, frost bites, minor flesh wounds, falls, injuries to the eyes, and even minor epidemics of influenza, grip and the like.

The hospital is not large—it has an area of 156 square feet—but it is admirably suited to its purpose, and equipped to meet any emergency not involving a great number of persons. Public health officials of the United States Government have inspected it, and pronounced it perfect in its details and more than adequate. Frequent use of the hospital was not anticipated, but THE NEWS felt that its employment in one serious emergency, when a life might depend upon it, was ample warrant for its installation.

The trained nurse not only administers first aid treatment but exercises a fine influence as an adviser in matters of health. At night the employes have the advantage of the attendance of a physician at all times. The varied personnel of a metropolitan newspaper is such that THE NEWS has on its staff, assisting in the publication of the paper, a doctor, a pharmaceutical chemist and a pharmacist.

The Hospital Is Equipped for Any Emergency.

THE NEWS has gone a little beyond the accepted high standards in providing the auxiliaries of health, cleanliness and comfort. There is a barber shop for executives. Shower baths are provided for all mechanics engaged in heavy or dirty work. All the air that is breathed in the building is washed and, in the colder seasons, tempered. Drinking water is softened, filtered, sterilized by ultra violet rays, and subjected to an artificial refrigerating process. Illumination is indirect, insuring a minimum strain upon the eyes at night; and the natural light of daytime is as near perfection as could be asked. Nowhere in the building are desks or machines placed against walls. All janitor work is done at night, with the aid of a complete vacuum cleaning system.

All in all, THE NEWS affords its employes not only an efficient plant with which to produce newspapers, but a most gratifying environment—an environment that, indeed, adds not only to the happiness but to the productivity of the staff.

THE POWER PLANT.

THE DETROIT NEWS has the distinction of being the one newspaper in the country—and very likely the world—which has within its own walls a remote control substation for the supplying of electrical power. This substation, contrary to former practices in power transmission, operates without an attendant.

The company which supplies THE NEWS with all of its electricity generates alternating current, direct current generation being restricted to a small amount for residence and retail business districts only. THE NEWS required direct current, however, and under ordinary circumstances would have had to draw this from the network of wires that underlies the business district and is fed from substations, more or less remote, where alternating current had been rectified to direct current. The power company figured that it could transmit to THE NEWS its block of power as alternating current and rectify this to direct current on the premises with greater over-all efficiency than by transmitting it as direct current.

The service is now transmitted to THE NEWS building at a pressure of 4,600 volts. It is then reduced in voltage through "step down" transformers, from which it flows to a rotary converter of 500 kilowatts (approximately 700 horse power) capacity. From this converter the direct current energy is obtained for use in motors and lamps at the usable voltage of 240 and 120. THE NEWS consumes in the neighborhood of 400 horse power, leaving 300 for general distribution.

THE NEWS is protected against mishap to its power. If the alternating current operating the rotary converter were cut off, the newspaper service would be fed through the direct current network.

No operating force is required for starting, stopping or regulating the supply of current, and the substation may be kept locked, being visited only at intervals for purposes of inspection. It is controlled from a station some distance away, and is automatically protected in case of disturbance on the system or accidents to the machine itself.   The economy of this system is obvious, especially as it bears upon the reduction of labor cost and the elimination of heating expense.

In the sub-basement which houses the sub-station, provision has been made for the storage of fuel and the installation of boilers should THE NEWS at any time choose to heat its own plant instead of bringing in steam provided by a central heating company.   Here also are vacuum cleaner pumps, air pumps, sumps, water heaters, steam controls and by-passes, emergency water supply tanks for the stereotyping department, house water tanks and such other mechanical equipment as is needed.

Elsewhere below ground is a room where are to be found all the meters in the building, easily accessible to inspectors and involving no inconvenience to employes.

This Vast Advertising Department Is Paralleled by a Circulation Department of Nearly Equal Size.

It Was an Innovation to Locate the Business Offices on the Second Floor.

THE BUSINESS OFFICES.

NO amount of glamor thrown around the gathering and writing of news can obscure the fact that newspaper publishing is an industry; that it entails prodigious labor in the fields of production and distribution, and that this labor must be wisely, effectively, economically directed. When the founder dreamed of a four-page newspaper with a maximum circulation of 10,000 copies daily, administrative problems were comparatively easy of solution, and scant space and little help were needed to manage the plant; but today, with 225,000 papers streaming from the shipping room each twenty-four hours, the demands are enormous.

In designing the new home of THE NEWS, it was determined very early that favored position should be given to the press, mailing and shipping departments in order that the paper might be handled efficiently and rapidly; that light and ventilation might be perfect for the workmen, and that at the same time the presses might be arranged so that their impressive magnitude would furnish the public with an unending spectacle. The ground floor alone satisfied the need. And yet, every tradition of newspaperdom had it that space on the main floor must be reserved for the business offices to insure ready access for the public to the department with which it has most business. With some trepidation, the publishers decided to put the business offices on the second floor; instantly a multitude of advantages were apparent, chief of which was the inter-relation of departments through the offices of the business manager, general manager, vice-president and editor, which lie at the point of contact between the editorial and business departments, the vice-president's office forming the connecting link. As for those of the public who visit the building, perfect elevator service was provided, and a complaint against this novel arrangement has never been heard.

More than a hundred employes, of diverse activities, are occupied with the problems of advertising, circulation and administration, and, in addition to ample working space for them, it was necessary to provide a generous area for those who wish to transact their business with THE NEWS over the counter. So the room is a very large one—eighty by one hundred and fifty-four feet—and constantly filled with the agreeable drone of business places.

43

The public entrance is not unimpressive. The office lobby is wide-sweeping, and is defined by oak-sheathed octagonal columns, with delicately carved capitals. At the left runs the advertising counter, at the right the circulation counter, the two terminating at the cashier's "cage" midway down the room. The coffered ceiling is cream-buff, to assist in the diffusion of light from indirect-ray fixtures, and rich stippled coloring fills the intermediate wall space between ceiling and high oak wainscoting.

The large amount of accounting done in the room occasioned particular attention to day as well as night illumination. The circulation department looks out upon the court above the shipping room, and its windows run the entire length of the room; the advertising department is located on the Second Avenue side, and has the full, fine light that the architecture permits. At no time between sunrise and sunset is artificial lighting necessary in any part of the business office,—true, indeed, of every working part of the building except the basement.

A reception room in charge of an information clerk is located near the entrance, inside the business office, and from here the visitor is directed to the department heads with whom he may have business. With the exception of circulation manager and the cashier, all such executives have offices on the advertising side of the room, running down the outer wall from the administrative suite. These offices are separated, not by walls but by waist-high partitions and railings, pierced by gates; the single exception being the office of the business manager, which adjoins the administrative suite. Next to the business manager, with whom he must frequently communicate, is the auditor, in whose department all purchases are handled, all disbursements audited, financial statements prepared and general business recorded.

Beyond are the advertising offices, including the foreign, local display and classified departments. The latter two are given large areas, their individual staffs consisting of some twenty men, whose duty it is not only to sell space but to maintain relations of amity and confidence between advertisers and the newspaper.

Thirty trunk lines, controlling a hundred and twenty-five telephone instruments, are employed by THE NEWS; and of these much the larger percentage serve the business offices.

Sixteen girls are concerned solely with the taking of classified advertisements over the telephone; and for their use a special, complex order table was devised.

Three hundred and eighty-seven "liner" advertising stations in the city must be called every day from the telephone table to insure the printing of all classified advertisements deposited with them, and while this is a huge task, it reduces materially the difficulties of the public in inserting advertisements, and lessens the number of telephone calls handled through THE NEWS exchange.

When the editorial department has completed the gathering and printing of its news, it is done with the paper which it has filled. No such good fortune for the advertising department, which furnishes the news of the world of commerce; the messages of those who have something to sell and those who are eager to buy. There are records to be kept of contracts made, of space consumed under these contracts, and of amounts due; there are bills to be made out after the difficult task of determining the applicable rate in each instance is completed, and there is the posting of the ledgers from these bills. There are collections to be made, and accounts to be settled as between the collector and the cashier.

All this means a very large allotment of space to the bookkeepers, billing clerks, collectors and stenographers who handle the advertising accounts and correspondence. This becomes still more obvious when it is recalled that THE DETROIT NEWS reached, in 1916, the position of first in America (which means in the world) in advertising, and that it increased its volume still further in 1917, attaining the remarkable total of 19,658,770 lines of paid advertising.

For a considerable time, in the early days of THE NEWS, the advertising was "farmed out" as a concession, and this, together with the modest proportions of the advertising as well as editorial pages, made office management a slight problem. But now there are thousands of advertising accounts to be kept, ranging from the myriad "liners" and the transient one-inch advertisement to the department store contract involving thousands of dollars a month; and there are perplexing schedules to be observed, governing the time of insertion and the location of advertising.

When the editorial and advertising departments have assembled the reading matter of the newspaper, and the presses have at last ground their grist, in steps the circulation manager to market the product. His chief problems are transportation and salesmanship, and neither is a trifling one when 225,000 patrons demand the paper, and must be served with speed and certainty. It will not do to publish less than are desired by the public; and, especially now when paper is so scarce, there must be no over-production. Maintenance of a fine balance between demand and supply calls for a large and expert staff, perfect organization and costly equipment.

The distributing organization of THE NEWS includes four thousand boys who sell or carry the paper in Detroit, and more than three thousand others who handle it throughout Michigan, Ohio and Ontario. Twelve hundred news stands and ninety supply stations in the city, as well as nine hundred and fifty state agents, have a hand in circulating THE NEWS. The efforts of all of these must be supported and directed from the circulation manager's desk in the business office, and this necessitates an independent corps of stenographers, clerks and bookkeepers.

Modern methods of circulation have reduced the office labor materially. Subscribers are no longer known in person to the editor, or the publisher, as was once the case with even some metropolitan papers. THE NEWS handles its city circulation of 180,000 through substations and division managers, who keep their individual accounts and report only in the large to the circulation department. Once THE NEWS had thousands of accounts to keep—one for every person who engaged to buy three or more papers.

The circulation manager of THE NEWS is relieved of one disagreeable and burdensome task, thanks to the policy of the paper. He does not have to handle premiums or run contests, nor does he employ canvassers. Without indulging in these questionable means of promoting circulation, the paper has increased its sales fifty thousand in three years.

Three departments are directly involved in distribution—the general office of the circulation department; the mailing room, where the papers are received fresh from the presses and bundled for delivery; and the shipping room, where forty-one automobiles maneuver briskly for positions at the loading platforms, ready to carry the papers to newsboy, news stand, interurban car, steam train or boat. Naturally, the circulation manager is the responsible head of all these agencies of distribution, and has frequent occasion to move from one to the other. To facilitate his movements, a one-man, pneumatic elevator is provided. It is concealed behind a secret door in the wainscoting, a step from his desk, and descends directly to the mailing room. The equipment and operation of the mailing and shipping rooms are described in another chapter.

The neatness of this, as of other departments of the plant, might lead one to forget the night and day forces of the building superintendent, whose office is across the corridor from that of the business manager. He has a staff of thirty whose duty is the maintenance of order and repair, and the protection of the building.

Apart from the general offices, but on the same floor, is the source of the unbelievable amount of sundries and printing necessary to the operation of the plant—the receiving and supplies department. System is the by-word of the department; the orders of the business manager its gospel. Not only does the custodian receive and check out all materials, from pen points to typesetting machines, but he operates the job printing plant and bindery which furnishes all departments with stationery, contracts, order blanks and other necessary printed matter. More than six hundred type forms are "kept standing," ready for use as various stocks become depleted. The money invested in the equipment and reserves of this room would capitalize a substantial mercantile house.

Altogether, the business department has been most generously dealt with in matters of space, convenience of arrangement and abundance of office accessories; and a considerable multiplication of its tasks as new opportunities are seized will not be embarrassing.

THE EDITORIAL OFFICES.

NO newspaper whose organization is fundamentally sound and whose permanent success is assured forgets that its keystone is competence in the gathering and disseminating of news, and sagacity in its interpretation. The dependability, the integrity of its editorial columns always constitutes its chief asset, and it strives ever to maintain the closest touch with its readers with a view to unvarying command of their confidence. The development of the modern metropolitan newspaper has been such as to lessen, however, the intimate personal contact of editor and reader. There are no Horace Greeleys today, maintaining open house for an eager and cozening public; they would have no time for their arduous duties. THE NEWS had this in mind in offering a certain degree of seclusion to its chief executives, yet maintaining accommodations which offer courtesy and comfort to those who come on errands and quests without number.

All business with the public is transacted on the second floor of THE NEWS building, and the architecturally superb lobby to which the elevator brings the visitor offers the most convenient possible access to the editorial reception room, as well as the business offices. No matter what his mission, if it but have to do with the news and editorial columns of the paper, the guest of THE NEWS, the least and the greatest alike, is given audience by pleasant and resourceful attendants.

Though the varied interests of the patrons of THE NEWS were constantly in view in the planning of the building, it was also necessary to consider the maintenance of an effective arrangement for the employes. Both factors had to do with the providing of individual entrances to the society and sport departments. A wholly feminine surrounding is afforded those who call on society's missions; and the great numbers of amateurs who bear tidings of the lesser athletic stars are offered a reception room off the workshop of the sporting editor, who has, of course, private access to the telegraph room and the general editorial offices. The claims of the friends of these two departments to time and attention are not to be gainsaid; and they were saved the discomfiture of intrusion upon the editorial staff congregated at its labors.

48

The casual and uncertain visitor enters the editorial reception room and has his needs attended to there.   Because it is neither conducive to efficient endeavor on the part of the staff nor the convenience of the public, few pass beyond; yet there is no holy of holies within—merely a suite where the members of the editorial staff daily reduce the complexities of life to their graphic elements.

Straight ahead of the entering visitor, through a doorway and across a narrow corridor which runs to right and left, lies a room occupied by the managing editor and so arranged that he may survey or pass to the two principal divisions of the department.   One is devoted to the editorial writers, critics, special writers and investigators; the other to those whose function it is to deal with the "breaking news," the immediate and palpitating "story," fresh from telegraph or telephone or the lips of an actor in some tremendously real tragedy, comedy or melodrama.

The special writers' room is but a step across a private corridor from the office of the editor, who is not only charged with the entire editorial management of the paper, but personally directs the work of the editorial writers. The room is peculiarly fitted for studious and unhurried effort.   Out of the main currents of traffic within the building, its occupants are saved from distractions of every sort.   It is sufficiently commodious to permit of wide spacing of the desks, so that a semi-seclusion is afforded each worker.   The north wall is as nearly solid glass as the architecture will permit, and the even light, without sun glare, is advantageous for habitual readers.   And this agreeable light sweeps across the room to the long south wall where, to a height of six feet, are book cases containing a thousand or more volumes of special reference works supplied for the exclusive use of the occupants of the room.

The cloistered atmosphere vanishes when one passes from this to the news room.   There if the machinery does not roar, it certainly hums; although it is not to be supposed that there is confusion.

Close to the managing editor's door, where his quick counsel may be had in the day's numerous emergencies, is a great "U" desk, or "horseshoe" at which ten executives and copy readers are seated, checking over and evaluating the news that constantly flows in upon them.   Here comes practically all the content of the newspaper, with the exception of advertising, editorials, and occasional privileged manuscript, or "copy," as it is called, from special writers.   It is the obligation of the copy readers to make perfect that which contains a flaw; to improve in grace or pungency of expression; to reduce in bulk, that the public may speedily and with pleasure consume the world's history for a day. Few realize that newspapers throw away more than they have room to print. The copy having been edited, a headline must be written; and of all the tasks of composition in a newspaper office this is the most exacting, and must be done under the greatest pressure.

Time was when every reporter was a writer. All are able to write with facility, but in this day of vast cities, long distances between points of action and the newspaper office, and frequently appearing editions, not every reporter can take the time to come into the office to weave into a fine fabric the elements of his story. There are, indeed, men who see little of the inside of their plant; reporters assigned to "beats" or "runs," whose constant presence at centers of news like the county building, the municipal courts and the police headquarters is essential, indeed necessary. The telephone solves their problem, but entails in the inner organization of the newspaper the appointment of what are known as rewrite men. They take over the wire the details the reporter has uncovered, and hastily transform their notes into the copy which is to be whisked from typewriter to copy desk and from copy desk to composing room. An inter-communicating telephone system makes it possible for the city editor, the rewrite man and the reporter to carry on a conversation at one time by phone, thus insuring dispatch in the handling of the news and co-ordination of effort.

About the spacious room are department editors and reporters, each with his individual desk and typewriter, the latter disappearing when not in use, but usually adding its whirr and click to the medley of undertones. For punctuation there is now and then the explosive arrival of proofs in a leather cartridge expelled from a pneumatic tube running from the composing room; or the sustained hiss as the copy readers' product is shot upward through the same ingenious and efficient carrier, to be hastily translated into type.

Were alacrity a characteristic of messenger boys, their services would still be altogether too slow for the bringing of telegrams to a metropolitan newspaper office. The labor cost of messengers may be judged from the fact that the private telegrams to THE NEWS average 9,146 words a day, and to this the three great news agencies serving the paper add 68,500 words which come from every part of the world over leased wires.

In the Editorial Department the Complexities of Life Are Reduced to Their Graphic Elements.

The Conference Room Is the Social Center of the Building.

For the handling of this vast amount of telegraphic news, provision is made for twelve telegraphers in a soundproof room adjoining the news room. The instruments are so constantly in use that their chatter is the most characteristic sound and distraction in newspaperdom. Both the editorial staff and those who "pound the brass" profit by the seclusion of the operators.

The exchange department is also given its mead of privacy, but for another reason. To the several members of this staff come hundreds of magazines and newspapers each day, and the constant mutilation of these publications results, perforce, in a somewhat littered room in the heat of the day's work. Large desks are necessary in order that the journals received may be spread for easy reading, clipping and pasting; and extraordinarily strong light is provided because of the quantity of finely printed matter that must be read. Segregation insures against a semblance of disorder in the news room, where otherwise the exchange department must have been located. Incidentally, in this day of the conservation of paper "exchange" is a misnomer, for newspapers buy the publications they desire to peruse, and send only to those who pay.

A stairway leads directly from the news room to the library and the reference room, those highly important accessories which lend authority to the hastily assembled articles that go to make up the newspaper. They are located on the mezzanine floor, so that they are at once accessible and free from the fevered spirit of those diligently bent on newspaper production. The passageway is for the exclusive use of the editorial department, and makes possible the utilization of the reading room as a lounge and study for the staff during intervals of inactivity. As situated, the library and reference room will never suffer abuse as a runway to any other part of the building, for only the offices of the president share the mezzanine floor with them.

The library contains ten thousand volumes, and acquisitions average a hundred a month. The books were selected by a scholarly veteran of the editorial force with the double view of supplying needed information under any emergency wherein a book might serve, and of furnishing to the staff interesting, practical and cultural reading along a widely inclusive range of subjects. The discursive student finds here a precious refuge from the world, or an open door to the most vital and immediate social, political and economic problems. But like the good city editor, intent upon discovering where important events are most likely to occur, the librarian and his assistants have endeavored to fortify themselves against a

Telegraphic Dispatches to THE NEWS Exceed 75,000 Words a Day.

sudden demand for books regarding hitherto uncultivated sources of news—strange lands, sequestered communities, expanding and significant movements among men, latest fields of exploitation. Elaborate analytical indexing makes the most elusive item in the library readily available.

Every encyclopedia of standing, special or general, is included in the library if it offers the slightest promise of usefulness; but the master encyclopedia for newspaper purposes is the reference department (long known as "the morgue," in journalistic jargon). With every edition that is emitted by the presses come additions to the stores of knowledge here contained; for the reference department's function is to clip and file in the most effective manner all the information that is likely ever to be of use again. Nor is it confined in selection to the newspaper it serves: whatever of value comes to the newspaper in public or private prints is here filed away to await the day of need. It is a living encyclopedia, always being brought down to date by a large and industrious staff of filing experts and trained newspaper men.

The content of the reference department is of three kinds: engravings, or "cuts," ready for instant insertion in the paper; photographs of persons, places and things, capable of being reproduced by the photo-engraving process within a few minutes; and facts and opinions on everything conceivably interesting to newspaper readers.

Four hundred and eighteen steel filing cabinets house this material, and have a capacity of 1,256 feet—nearly a quarter of a mile—of envelopes. Data and pictures touching approximately 60,000 subjects or persons were preserved from the vast accumulation in the old building; and to these are added normally about 500 subjects a month. Engravings number about 25,000, though twice that number were weeded out when THE NEWS moved. Obviously, intelligent elimination is an important duty of the director and his associates, for the department might easily be cluttered beyond all reason with unavailable material.

Closely allied with the library and reference room is the file room, where in fireproof cabinets are kept the bound volumes of THE NEWS from its inception, August 23, 1873, to the present day. They are the most precious treasure of the institution, and the privilege of their use is closely restricted. In them lie the history, in editorial, story and advertisement, not only of a rarely successful newspaper, but of a great city in its most fascinating half century.

THE ART DEPARTMENT.

THE room occupied by the art department is unique in at least one respect: it was surrendered by architect and decorator to the devices of its occupants, and they plunged into the considerable task of painting murals depicting stages in the development of pictorial art. These murals will ultimately cover one hundred and eighty feet of wall space, and include portrayals of the artist at work from the stone age, through the Assyro-Babylonian, Egyptian, Greek, Roman, Byzantine, medieval and modern periods. Spaced through will be pictures illustrative of the achievements of the Japanese and Chinese, as well as of such primitive folk as the Indian and the Eskimo.

Departing from the commoner method, the art staff has painted in oil directly on the plaster, instead of on canvas or paper for subsequent mounting upon the walls; and the murals will endure as long as does the building. The artists set for themselves a narrow range of color, running from Delft blue to cream-buff, and within this attained exceedingly attractive results in something akin to poster tones. They also had the wood-work and furniture refinished in the key of the pictures, to achieve the effect desired in the room.

Accommodations for the art staff are, undoubtedly, without an equal in the newspaper world. The department was allotted three thousand two hundred square feet of floor space, one thousand five hundred of which is for the cartoonists and illustrators. The latter space is especially attractive since twelve desks may be located at as many windows, all with the desirable north light, without inconvenience of any kind.

Three drawing tables have been provided for each pair of artists, so that the presentation of a new task or problem does not necessitate the sweeping away of one layout to permit the spreading of the new. This is of especial importance to the men whose duty it is to handle layouts for the rotogravure and other Sunday sections, and it adds at least twenty-five per cent to the efficiency of the staff.

Two tables six feet long are provided for laying out work, and between them is a specially conceived and constructed supply table, with concealed paste pots and sink for soaking photographs—usually the most unsightly things in an art department. Multiplied use of the air brush and pantograph, which is in itself a highly desirable end, will result from the permanent attachment of these instruments to one of the tables.

Elaborate filing systems have been provided for the preservation of drawings which are in frequent use; roller files for rotogravure and art pages; a safe for valuable camera lenses, and abundant space for art studies, general literature, catalogues and correspondence.

Each drawing table has a special tool drawer with partitions and slide trays to induce neatness and system, as well as larger drawers for the storing of the individual artist's personal files, portfolio and reference works.

Intercommunication with the engraving department, where all pictures must go, is perfect; and easy access to the composing room and the editorial departments is afforded. Only a partition separates the desks of the head of the engraving department and the director of the art department; and of course that is pierced by a door through which interdepartmental traffic is handled.

To some the most fascinating portion of the department, in many respects the most original in arrangement, is that occupied by the photographers.

Newspaper photography's increasing importance, especially now that the processes of reproduction have approached perfection in the rotogravure section, warranted special attention to the needs of the "camera men." The newspaper of today goes beyond the mere publication of pictures with news value, and actually ventures into the field of pure art. Portraiture of a high order also makes notable demands upon the newspaper's space, especially on Sundays.

More than half of the forty by eighty foot room set aside for the art department is consumed by the photographers, to whom are granted a gallery, a developing and printing room, a work room, a dressing room, an office, and filing cabinet space. The gallery and dressing room are for the convenience of those who are photographed while visiting the newspaper offices, for purposes of publication.

The gloom that customarily attends workmen in darkrooms is here dispelled by buff-tinting the interior. The developing, printing and enlarging rooms are sealed against the intrusion of daylight, so that the rays that are reflected from the pleasantly toned interior walls are exclusively artificial and, when desirable, harmless in color. All direct entrances to these workrooms are furnished with sliding doors. Indirect entrances are jet black mazes which daylight cannot traverse.

The photographers are not confined to interior work, although the gallery is abundantly lighted by windows and mercury lamps. The art department is immediately beneath the roof of the building, which is accessible, and admirably adapted to outdoor photography, especially speed work when the object is in motion. Portable lights are available for small flashlight pictures when the members of the staff are required to do interior work away from the building, and an automobile is provided for their exclusive use.

There are numerous occasions when newspaper photographers are required to perform miracles of speed, especially on such occasions as the arrival of distinguished visitors to the city, accidents, mid-day parades and gigantic assemblies. Then of all times the photographers appreciate their advantages. Their present record is the development of six plates and the making of four enlargements in twenty minutes—a practical demonstration of the fact that esthetic surroundings have not reduced the efficiency of the artists.

The Newspaper of Today Actually Ventures into the Field of Pure Art.

The Composing Room Is Extraordinarily Efficient in Arrangement and Equipment.

Engraving and Intaglio Printing.

THE illustrating of a newspaper was anything but a fine art when THE DETROIT NEWS first appeared. In fact, nearly a decade passed before anything but the most meager attempt was made to satisfy the public's desire for things pictorial. A borrowed engraving was sometimes employed, on such an occasion as the burning of a locally famous church; otherwise cuts were restricted to crude ones employed in equally crude advertisements.

THE NEWS was by no means slow to realize the need of, or reluctant to take the lead in, illustration. The difficulty was the tardiness of inventors in supplying practicable means of engraving for the daily press. Ultimately THE NEWS made rapid strides in the enlivening of its pages with pictures; and in this respect it has always led in the vast community it has served. Indeed, coming down to the present day, it was the first newspaper in the state to give its subscribers a roto-gravure section, and the first (in fact, at present the only one) to install in its own plant a complete equipment for production of this finest type of newspaper pictorial art.

All the perfection of modern newspaper illustration is due to the development since the eighties of the photo-engraving process. THE NEWS began experimenting with it at the dawn of the nineties; and in 1895 had within its own walls a complete engraving plant.

Prior to the development of photo-engraving, the old chalk plate held sway. It was a simple method of engraving, fairly rapid and not unworthy. A coating of chalk, magnesia and gelatine was spread upon a steel plate and baked to hardness. The artists scratched their pictures through the chalk, after which stereotypers used the plate as a mould into which they poured metal. The penetration of the molten metal to the steel base, wherever the artist scratched a line, resulted in a raised surface on the block of type metal which, when cool, came from the casting box. This raised surface took the ink and left its imprint on the newspaper, exactly as does type.

The great advantages of photo-engraving which led to its general adoption by the press were not only its equal or greater speed and finer quality, but its elasticity, for it admits of enlarging or reducing pictures to any desired size, either to fit a given space or to harmonize with other pictures; and it also makes possible, as the chalk plate process did not, the almost perfect reproduction of photographs.   The best an artist could do in earlier days was to scratch through the chalk a picture sketched from the original photograph.

Completeness, compactness, economy and facility were developed in the layout and equipment of the new engraving department.   It lies in a brilliantly lighted corner of the building, adjoining the art department, whence its photographs and drawings come, and is but a step from the composing room, to which the finished cuts must go.   Three of the four walls are largely glass, affording the utmost usable daylight; but because the work of the engravers must be done at all hours of day and night, and under all conditions of weather, the natural light is not depended on by the camera operators, but is augmented by seven powerful arc lamps whose intensity is constant.   Skylights have no place in the department, their fickleness having been demonstrated years ago.

Representative of the modern character of all the appurtenances of the department are the vacuum printing and etching machines.   In printing photographs on metal the air is exhausted between the glass plate and the zinc or copper sheet, and atmospheric pressure makes the contact perfect and unvarying. The etching machines are huge square tubs made of glazed crockery in which paddles splash a fine spray of acid against the metal plates.   These machines are imported from Sweden, and represent the rather uncommon items in the equipment of THE NEWS building which cannot be obtained from American manufacturers.   The expense of installation is warranted in view of the fact that the two hours consumed in the "acid bath" in the old fashioned wooden rocker-tub is now reduced to forty minutes, even when a full-page cut is being etched.

In an emergency, the engraving department can produce from a photograph, by the halftone photo-engraving process, a cut, ready to print, in twenty-one minutes.   Such speed is not productive of engravings of consistently high quality, and is not ordinarily attempted.

A romantic element in the equipment of the department is the proof press, operated by hand, which is identical in principle and almost so in construction with the printing presses at which Benjamin Franklin toiled in his youth.

Rotogravure, or intaglio printing is still in its infancy, and has been in use in American newspapers only a half dozen years; but the fidelity of reproductions to the original photographs, the perfect texture of the pictures from shadow to high light, have added new qualities to newspaper illustration, and the process

Tons of History Were Written in Picturesque Old Editorial Rooms.

Forty-Four Years of History Were Written in the Picturesque Old Editorial Rooms.

is certain to persist. Its instant appeal to the readers was obvious, and resulted in a clamor for space in the rotogravure section for the publication of new and unusually attractive types of advertising.

One expects, in the rotogravure department, to come upon an amazingly complex printing press, whereas in fact it is remarkable rather for its simplicity. Yet it was the imperfection of the presses and not the intricate and costly process of engraving that retarded the development of this fine addition to the newspaper until a half dozen years ago. In its essence, the rotogravure press consists of nothing more than a fragile looking machine at either end of which, close to the floor, are a large and a small cylinder. The former bears the engraved copper printing surface; the latter is an impression cylinder. The engraved cylinder revolves in a trough, or fountain, of thin sepia-toned ink. The ink is scraped off the non-printing surface of the plate by a beveled steel knife, just before it comes in contact with the paper, insuring a perfect deposit of only that ink which is contained in the depressions, and which is requisite to the reproduction. Between the impression and printing cylinders runs the ribbon of paper which, after being printed, passes through two ovens, over a steam drum and into the folder which delivers it dry, properly trimmed and ready for immediate use, at a rate of 7,200 copies an hour.

No stereotyping interposes between the engraving of a rotogravure plate and the printing of the finished section. The cylinder is steel, but receives by electrolytic process a coating of about three-eighths of an inch of copper to which the pictures are transferred and on which they are etched by various acids of secret formulae. When the printing process has been completed, the cylinder can be planed down about a sixty-fourth of an inch, and used again. A cylinder can be used ten or twelve times without replating.

The handling of the photographs from the time they leave the art department till they are engraved upon the copper involves high skill in photography and chemistry, and is difficult of description. There are hardly a score of experts in rotogravure work in the country; and THE NEWS is fortunate in possessing the services of one who was among the first Americans to develop mastery of the craft.

So long as engraving served only the purposes of crude illustration, it was of no great importance to the daily press; but now its uses are almost unlimited in the newspaper's business of transmitting information and opinion. That intaglio printing should also please the esthetic sense and thus be a stimulus to endeavor in the field of art is an added reason for its inclusion in such a newspaper as THE NEWS aims to be.

THE COMPOSING ROOM.

GREAT are the changes that have come over the personnel of the composing room in the last generation. The printer is, today as yesterday, an intellectual aristocrat among tradesmen by virtue of his inevitable contact with a wide range of information; but today he is distinguished as well for his stability and poise, whereas yesterday he was very often a romantic and fascinating bird of passage, restlessly weaving his way to and fro across the country, accumulating vast stores of interesting if not important information, and developing a fine genius in his handicraft.

A veteran member of the staff of THE NEWS remembers vividly a sign posted in a boarding house window near the old plant: "Boarders wanted; no cobblers or printers." A hint of amiable weaknesses, peculiar to those journeymen craftsmen who vanished before the typesetting machine, and are no more. The compositor of this generation must lead an ordered life to lend himself successfully to the tremendous and spirited battle against time, involved in newspaper production.

Nowhere in a newspaper plant is a more insistent demand for speed felt than in the composing and stereotyping departments. The editorial staff, having set its story upon paper, clamors for its appearance in the earliest possible edition; and the press room forces, always under obligation to release newspapers to the circulation department at a given minute—aye, second—cry for the printer to "close his forms" and for the stereotyper to cast his plates in order that the great rumbling presses may be at their task. With this pressure applied from two sides, these mechanical divisions of the publishing plant were naturally designed with especial view to efficient effort.

With approximately one hundred and twenty-five men employed in the composing room, obviously much attention had to be given to the allotment of space and to the location of the typesetting machines, thirty-seven in number, which mold into easily handled "slugs" the information offered the reader through the editorial and advertising departments. In double file, the linotypes are ranged along one whole side and end of the vast room, convenient to the sources of that copy which is to be reduced to type, and to the men who make up the pages of the newspapers. Twenty-four of the machines are devoted to editorial matter, and thirteen to advertising and job work.

In addition to the equipment mentioned, there are two machines for casting "slugs" for display advertising and such large type as is utilized in the caption of the newspaper.   Also there are two lead and rule casters, machines which make all of the borders, rules and dashes used in the newspaper.   These machines are not only economical of space and storage facilities, as well as of the time of the workmen, but they insure perfectly new, clean printing faces, in great variety and abundance.

The composing room is no maze of creaking belts and pulleys, or unsightly pipes and posts.   Every machine is motored—true, indeed, throughout the building—and equipped with an electric melting pot.   The water and electricity necessary to operation are conveyed in a covered trench that runs between the two columns of linotypes.

Each of the typesetting machines is capable of doing the work of five or six old-time hand compositors, and not only because of the necessity of maintaining a constant return upon the large investment, but because of the serious loss in product when a machine is out of order, an elaborate repair department is maintained.   At the junction of the columns of machines is the office of the highly skilled mechanics who are charged with the efficient upkeep of the typesetting devices.   The operator of a machine that suffers a tantrum is a highly paid workman, and must not be idle; nor must he take up his time with repair work at which he may be less skilled than the mechanics employed for such tasks.   He presses a button, and the signal reaches the repair department.   The mechanics, from their workshop, glance at an enunciator equipped with a red light for each machine, and observe which one is in trouble.   If the difficulty is serious, the operator is promptly assigned to a reserve machine.

Very little of the news matter appearing in a newspaper can be prepared more than a few hours before publication, so that full right of way must be given when copy begins pouring in each morning.   Consequently, as much advertising matter as possible is set in more leisurely hours, night and day forces being maintained.   The exigencies of newspaper making are such, also, that extra editions of the utmost importance may be called for at any hour of day or night—almost invariably without warning.   With competent workmen on hand at all times, the issuing of extras is ever possible with no disturbance to the normal organization of plant or staff.

No small part of the effort attendant upon newspaper production is that expended by the dozen proof readers, whose duty it is to guard against typographical errors in the publication. Not a line that appears in the newspaper, whether advertising, news or editorial comment, but is scanned by their vigilant eyes; and the marvel is not the multiplicity of jumbled letters or misplaced lines that persist in appearing, but their paucity. The human kind is prone to err, yet in THE NEWS the average of errors in typography is 1 to 3,250; that is to say, every character set offers an opportunity for error, yet only an insignificant number of faults are discernible.

Individual desks are furnished the proof readers, who are grouped about their chief near the center of the composing room. Abundant light is afforded by the monitors overhead and the almost solid walls of glass on the east and west sides of the great room. The customary seclusion of the proof room was avoided in the construction of the new building as inconvenient and without material advantage to the workmen.

To avoid any possible confusion in the handling of the varied matter which finds its way into the columns of the newspaper, distinct departments are established throughout the composing room where the type is handled until it is ready for the "forms" in which the pages are laid out. Ingenious systems have been devised to enable department heads to discover in a moment, as is often necessary, the exact status of the most complex piece of type composition. There was a day when foremen went clamoring about the composing room, vainly endeavoring to locate copy and type, especially when, as in the composition of advertisements, several hands were at the task.

Sunday newspapers have grown so large that no newspaper organization could handle all the parts in a single day. The work is distributed, in fact, throughout the week. Opportunities for confusion, especially in liner advertisements, are consequently multiplied; but in the new home of THE NEWS the complete separation of the Sunday and daily storage banks and classification departments prevents any conflict.

THE NEWS, in its new quarters, goes farther than any other paper in the country in the composition of advertising on linotype machines. It has, as a matter of fact, kept a step ahead of the manufacturers, forcing innovations from time to time. Every "ad" machine will set up to thirty-six point type, and the headline machines will set as high as forty-two point, the largest size employed in single column headlines on this newspaper. All "ad" machines are capable of setting as high as eighteen point type on solid bases—an important innovation from the printer's standpoint. All the linotypes are new and of the latest model, "double-, triple- and quadruple-deck, quick change" machines; that is, capable of shifting from one character of type to another in a moment, and without material effort. The few machines not especially purchased for the new building had been but recently installed in the old.

An unpretentious but exceedingly busy little department of the composing room is the mail list room, where two employes are kept constantly at work making changes in addresses of subscribers, and adding new names. From the circulation department revisions are received daily, and the corrections are instantly made. Only the mail list for one day is ever printed, lest there be a temptation to let a mistake be repeated and a paper go astray. The addresses are printed on a long strip of paper which is thrust into a machine that automatically clips and pastes the familiar little colored slip onto the wrapper or front page of the newspaper.

Large city newspapers with intensive local circulations make comparatively little use of the mails in distribution. Motor transports and express cars carry the bulk of out-of-town shipments. For this reason, THE NEWS mailing list includes only about six thousand names, despite the paper's dominant position in Michigan.

The day of the printer-editor is fast vanishing, but even the metropolitan editorial staff must be represented in the somewhat inky realms. The editors who have charge of the "makeup" of the reading matter must be in the composing room to direct the compositors. They are not permitted to handle any of the type, or to do anything except direct the mechanical staff in the arrangement of the content of the newspaper; but this task is in itself so large that it necessitates a secondary editorial office in the composing room. It is adjacent to the pneumatic tube, through which copy comes from the editorial department, and to the member of the composing room staff who, as "copy cutter," doles out the stories of the reporters to the linotype operators. The sub-editor in charge of this desk is able to supervise all copy before it goes to the machines.

With the opening of the new building and the printing of the first issue there, the readers of THE NEWS were introduced for the first time to a new style of type, which, though not appreciably larger, is made much more legible because of the greater space between lines. Nearly four inches less reading matter is contained in each column, but the costly sacrifice was made for the comfort of the reader's eyes.

THE STEREOTYPING DEPARTMENT.

IN 1880 THE NEWS installed its first web press and stereotyping outfit, a marvel of course in its day, and remembered affectionately by one of the present staff of stereotypers who was then an apprentice. The builder of the original equipment was Walter Scott, father of the manufacturer of the newly installed battery of presses.

In that distant day, the papier mache matrix, which receives the impression of the type and later becomes a mould from which the plates for the presses are cast, was beaten into the page of type with long-handled, flat-surfaced brushes. The wielding of these called for much dexterity and no little muscle. Today this work is done in the new building by moulding machines which exert a pressure of seven hundred pounds to the square inch on the soft, moist matrix, forcing it into all the interstices of the page of type as it passes under great steel rollers. The moisture is removed from the matrix by the use of electrically heated drying tables which exert a pressure of eleven tons and at the same time apply 350 to 400 degrees of heat, which is below the melting point of the type metal, and hence safe.

THE NEWS displaced the old "beating brushes" as far back as 1893, although in a much later period they were used in emergencies, and even regularly in a few metropolitan newspaper offices until the last decade. Many small papers still employ them. Prejudice against innovations, however logical and inevitable, operated to keep the brushes in use long after their day in the larger offices had passed.

The installation of the first moulding machines in Detroit had its humorous aspects, and was not the result of any eagerness on the part of newspapers to experiment with a still doubtful device. The old *Detroit Tribune* was at one time located across an alley from a famous hotel, and the night's repose of many a guest in an adjacent bedroom was disturbed by the battering of brushes against forms. The proprietors of the hotel paid the cost of the new equipment and hired an expert to demonstrate its use. Even so, when the tutor was gone the pupils slid back to the brushes, the plant organization being somewhat unsuitable to use of the machines. Later, when Mr. Scripps bought *The Tribune,* they were carted to the offices of THE NEWS where they were in use for many years.

When THE NEWS began stereotyping its pages, twelve plates constituted a good day's output for two men, and the week's total was customarily eighty plates. The three double automatic plate-casting and trimming machines in the new building are capable of turning out eighteen plates a minute. Six hundred plates are frequently cast in a day; seven hundred is not an uncommon number. Before trimming, a plate weighs eighty pounds, and all the metal that is cast must be rehandled to replenish the cauldrons; so the stereotypers on a week day must wrestle with fifty-six tons of metal. For Sunday issues they have made over twelve hundred plates on a Saturday and Saturday night, necessitating the handling of ninety-six tons of metal. A muscle-building task!

A smelting furnace of a type hitherto installed only in eastern newspaper establishments, operating at a temperature of 2,300 degrees, occupies a segregated room where dross is removed from the metal as it is used in the typecasting and stereotyping machines, over and over again. Faulty handling of metal results in tremendous wastage, and THE NEWS has aimed to eliminate as much of this as possible.

Smelters, ingot-casters and plate-casting machines all give off noxious gases, necessitating special and thorough ventilation. It was for this reason that THE NEWS, contrary to the practice in most newspaper plants, located the stereotyping department on the top floor so that the fumes from the metal pots might not drift through the building. However there is another advantage in the location of the stereotyping department beside the composing room. It permits of that economical circular movement of materials, raw to finished, which is one of the industrial fascinations of the building. As for the dispatching of plates to the press room, it is accomplished as easily as the commoner transportation of matrices. The casting equipment radiates from two automatic plate elevators which drop to air cushions, noiselessly, and deliver their burden directly to the plate conveyor in the press room, which carries them to the press for which they are intended.

The department is fully equipped for both news and job work with the latest devices; and all job machinery is present in duplicate to allow for severe pressure or the emergency of accident. Indicative of the modern character of the equipment is a laundry blanket-dryer capable of accommodating fifty-two of the thick woolen pads an hour, and eliminating the unsightly and inconvenient reminder of back yards on a Monday. Another installation of importance in this day is special mechanisms for the stereotyping of double-page plates, to accommodate advertisers who are no longer satisfied with a single-page "spread." Without this equipment stereotypers must resort to difficult and none too safe patchwork, and the results are never wholly satisfactory.

When THE NEWS first stereotyped its pages, four men sufficed to handle all the work of making the plates, running the presses and supplying the power. Two were stereotypers, one was a pressman and one a combination engineer, fireman and errand boy. The stereotypers turned in and aided the pressman when their own tasks were accomplished. Today the stereotyping department alone employs eighteen skilled workmen.

The Stereotypers Handle Fifty-Six Tons of Metal Daily.

The Presses Have a Capacity of 432,000 Sixteen-Page Papers an Hour

THE PRESS ROOM.

ALL the world thrills in the presence of any stupendous and perfect machine; and wherever newspapers expose their rumbling, racing presses to the public view, there will be found faces flattened against window panes and eyes rounded. In THE NEWS building not alone is the entire press and mailing room visible from the street, but a balcony projects from the mezzanine floor, whereon the thousand visitors who are guided through the building each month may stand and survey, with unobstructed view, a workplace half the size of the average city block.

When THE DETROIT NEWS was established in 1873, the "web perfecting press," a machine which would print both sides of the paper at once from a roll, or reel, of paper was but eight years old and in use in very few publishing plants. Its inventor, William A. Bullock, had been killed in one of his own presses two years after he devised it.

Mr. Scripps had to content himself in the beginning with an old four-cylinder press, purchased second hand and earning, before it was discarded, the epithet "the threshing machine." It is still the butt of office jokes, among those whose minds carry back over the intervening 38 years, but it served its purpose. And glamorous as was its history already, it was to pass on from Detroit to Toledo ; and from there to parts unknown, always helping to speed the printed word.

It was reputed to have a capacity of 15,000 papers an hour, but when accidents happened—as they frequently did—getting the 10,000 THE NEWS needed to satisfy its subscribers was a task that often carried on well into the night. Manipulating this press involved a considerable force of men, and what was well nigh a ritual. There was a man to feed each of the four cylinders, and the papers came forth unfolded, and printed on one side only, thus necessitating a second run. The newsboys for a time were required to fold their own papers. And damp, odoriferous papers they were, for the superstition still prevailed in practically all newspaper offices that the paper must be sprinkled to insure good printing.

In that day a circulation of 10,000 offered serious problems indeed, and the bulky Sunday or even daily newspapers of today were impossible of realization because of the amount of type to. be set, all by hand, and the difficulties incident to printing. By 1880, the old equipment had been proved inadequate and a web press, with a capacity of 30,000 four-page papers an hour, was obtained. Instantly the circulation shot up approximately 9,000, indicating plainly that the the demand had not been met theretofore. Today THE NEWS presses are capable of an output of 432,000 sixteen-page papers, printed, trimmed, folded, counted and delivered to the mailing department every hour—7,200 a minute! This exceeds present demands upon the equipment, but, recalling the remarkable advances of recent years, one can only dream what possibilities the future holds.

The color press, which does not pretend to be swift, is itself capable of printing comic supplements at a rate of 11,000 an hour, four colors at a time. The color sections, being called for but once a week and their content lacking the timeliness of news, need not be rushed through the presses in an hour or even a day. The color press is a turtle among hares, though in this tale the race always ends a tie on Sunday morning.

In no other part of a newspaper plant must expensive machinery lie idle so many hours of the day and night; but a press is like a fire engine, a fleet, an army—when it is called into service it must be prepared for a maximum effort, and it must be infallible.

Technically, the equipment would be spoken of as "two triple octuple presses," yet from the layman's point of view they could be considered either as one press or as twenty-four; for there are twenty-four units so consolidated as to make them one vast machine. These units are so interrelated that any one can be run or silenced at will, and can be operated separately or in connection with any other unit on the floor. Running a sixteen-page paper, the presses would operate as twelve quadruples, issuing 432,000 copies an hour. They would operate as eight sextuples on a twenty-four-page paper, with an output of 288,000 an hour; and as six octuples on a thirty-two-page edition, printing 216,000 an hour. Thus all units are constantly employed, whatever the size of the paper.

One needs to walk their length to sense how large the presses really are, for they are so finely proportioned to the spacious room that they do not at first impress one. They are 193 feet 2 inches long by approximately 20 feet wide, and are thrust 9 feet above the floor. In addition there is a nine-foot understructure of foundation frames and huge reels for the paper which feeds the presses. The order for these presses, the largest ever received by their makers, was placed in 1914, work was begun on them in 1915, and two years elapsed before construction and installation was completed.

The electrical equipment of the presses is the finest ever designed for any printing machinery. The control board, located on the mezzanine floor and visible through a glass partition, is 44 feet long by 7 feet high. It need never be approached by a pressman—a departure from anything ever built before for a publishing house. The control board automatically sets itself in accordance with the shifting of gears or clutches by the pressman to obtain the desired press combinations. The twelve motor equipments of the presses can be operated independently or in any desired combinations, and they are so arranged that a control panel or motor out of order can be eliminated at the presses and power drawn from another. Grounded wires, short circuits and other bugaboos of the user of electrical power have no terrors for THE NEWS pressmen, for inventive genius has prevented their ever interfering with the continuous operation of all parts of the printing equipment. Safety appliances are, of course, numerous and adequate.

The complete motorization of the plant has done something more than insure efficient operation. It has eliminated every sign of shafts, belts and pulleys, and made the workrooms safer and better to look upon. A long stride from the old seven horse-power donkey engine which furnished all the power in the original plant!

Upkeep of the presses necessitates equipment for all emergencies, and to this end THE NEWS maintains a remarkably complete machine shop in charge of a skilled press erector and machinist. He has in his domain drill presses, two great lathes, a shaper, a milling machine and a grinder, besides incidental small machinery and tools which enable him, if it were

The Press Control Board Is an Electrical Marvel.

necessary, to rebuild a press on the premises. No problem of machine work, whether on a motor, an automobile, or a printing press, is beyond this department's capacity.

Forests must die each day that the paper appears, for at the present time THE NEWS consumes every twenty-four hours, a hundred rolls of paper made from wood pulp; and each roll contains six miles of paper. The ribbon of paper is 71 inches wide, and races through the presses at the rate of 14,175 inches a minute, or 70,875 feet an hour. When all the presses are in operation they use 1,701,000 feet, or over 322 miles every hour. Last year, 219,000 miles of paper wended its inky way through the machinery—nine times enough to encircle the earth. A single daily edition of THE NEWS uses 104,700 pounds of paper, or more than 52 tons; and the Sunday edition uses over 125 tons, without counting wastage.

Paper famines are very real and very serious when the normal demands of a publication are such as this; and fluctuation even of a fraction of a cent a pound is a matter of grave concern.

In the basement is a great concrete storage pier, 147 feet wide and 50 feet deep, whereon the day's supply is kept, together with two days' reserve. A paper storage warehouse is now in process of construction on property adjoining the site of THE NEWS, which the paper recently acquired. This building will have a capacity of twelve thousand full rolls—a four months' supply at the present rate of consumption. Warehouses elsewhere in the city contain the vast supplies which safeguard THE NEWS meantime, and these are tapped to keep the storage pier in the basement filled.

The loading of the pier is the first step in the efficient circular movement of the bulky raw material of the newspaper. The paper arrives on trucks, in the shipping room, and is lifted by electric hoists and dropped into a paper tunnel through which it rolls, on an elevated runway, to scales. After being weighed, it is rolled onto high iron cradle-trucks running on a miniature railway track the full width of the pier, and deposited where needed. This pier is twenty-two inches high at the back, and slopes toward the presses, where it is but eleven inches above floor level. The paper is thus able to move forward without involving man-power. Low trucks receive the rolls when they are called for, and speed them along supply tracks which completely loop the twenty-four magazine reels which supplement the press units.

Magazine Reels Make Possible the Changing of Paper Rolls Without Stopping the Presses.

The Storage Platform Must Yield 219,000 Miles of Paper to the Presses Each Year.

The delays once incident to the removal of an empty spindle shaft and the substitution of a new roll of paper are no more known to THE NEWS. Double three-arm "spiders" are employed which, operated electrically, relieve the employes of the hard task of hoisting rolls of paper weighing three-quarters of a ton. These magazine reels, the latest press room device of importance, are so constructed that while the press is being fed by one roll of paper, another fresh one is ready for automatic attachment to the fleet, taut web of paper, and the third depleted roll is at the exact height necessary to be removed and replaced by a full roll without any lifting or straining upon the part of the workmen. Stopping the presses is unnecessary. The cost of these reels would, in itself, fully equip a substantial, small-city newspaper; and the sole objects of the investment were speed and the elimination of man-handling of the ponderous rolls.

Half a ton of ink is consumed daily by the presses, and the handling of it is a more or less serious and disagreeable problem. Ink has an affinity for dirt, and, caught on the sole of a shoe, will travel as far and mar as much as pine pitch. Exposed to the air it will gather unbelievable quantities of dust, lint from paper, and other foreign substances which interfere with good printing. To obviate the necessity of straining the ink and of cleansing the press fountains periodically of a gummy residue of ink and dirt, an ingenious system was devised.

An air-tight tank trailer, resembling a street sprinkler, follows a motor truck to the ink factory, where it is attached to a tank into which the ink mills have emptied their product. Compressed air forces the ink into the trailer, and it returns to THE NEWS where by the same process the ink is forced from the trailer to the storage tank in the basement. An ink closet with pipe connections is conveniently located in the shipping room, where the trailer may stand while unloading. From the storage tank, the ink is pumped into the sealed fountains in the presses, so that it never knows light of day or dust-laden air till it goes on paper. Clean, unblemished printing is the result.

The old-time picturesque tussle with papers in stacks of fifty, a hundred and two hundred, delivered at several decks on a towering press, is likewise done away with. It was pleasing to the artist to depict the lightly clad toilers, glistening with perspiration; some stooping with their load, others straining away to the insatiable mailing room. But the human element is again reduced. Continuous conveyors, in which the overlapping papers are held by coiled wire spring belts, take the papers directly from the presses, speed them aloft to the ceiling, straight across the room and down to the mailing department tables. The papers are

mechanically counted in fifties as they are delivered, then tied in packages by
workmen and heaved into knee-high bundle belt conveyors which find their way
out to the loading platform in the shipping room where numerous trucks awa
their burden.

Thus the elliptical movement is completed. The finished papers from the
presses have retraced, a floor above, the path followed by the rolls of print
paper, in the basement. In all the processes of conversion from the receipt of
spotless rolls to the whisking away of the news-laden papers, there is no unnecessary motion, no wasteful inch of travel. And only twice are the muscles of men
called upon to handle the paper—when the bundles are made up, and when
they are tossed into the truck to whose route they belong. It is the press room's
evidence of the efficiency of the entire organization of the plant.

THE MAILING AND SHIPPING ROOMS.

NERVOUS tension in a newspaper manufactory afflicts the mailing and shipping rooms last. But the moment the presses have sped themselves from a grumble to a roar, the stream of papers begins to flow across the room in the conveyors, and to count out its fifties at the thirty great steel tables on which the bundles are made. Mailers fall to their tasks. Drivers "tune up" their motors at the loading platform, awaiting the clumsy packages that will shortly be dumped forth from an endless belt. It is the last fight against time.

Despite the quantity of labor-saving devices installed in the mailing room, there is still work for more than two score men on the daily editions, and for eighty or more when the prodigious SUNDAY NEWS is accumulating. To these are added the truck drivers and their assistants, who, in the slack hours when no papers are being distributed, busy themselves with the "filling" of rotogravure and comic sections.

Ingenious as are the presses in the publishing plant of this day, they will not completely assemble the eighty-four or eighty-eight pages that go to make up the average edition of THE SUNDAY NEWS. Nor is it possible for most of the Sunday newspaper to be printed much in advance of the subscriber's morning exercise of bringing it in from the front porch. So this task of filling, or assembling the sections is one that calls for a throng of Saturday night workers, most of whom are employed elsewhere during the week and seize an opportunity to add to their incomes.

Quite different are these from the days when there was one regular mailing room hand and the rest, in charge of the commercial editor of the paper, were made up from the office force! Nor was it uncommon for the founder to appear in the midst of the workmen to help count the papers and direct the efforts of his employes.

Three or four years ago, edition time was marked by the assembling of a noisy band of newsies who bought their wares over the counter in a rude sales-room provided for their convenience. Their purchases commonly ran seven or eight thousand copies a day. The salesroom, magnified in attractiveness and convenience as well as size, is still provided, but few boys find it necessary to visit THE NEWS. Automobiles carry the papers all day to the youngsters in the very center of the city, and six make frequent trips to each of the street corners where sales are consistently large. The papers are thus kept constantly on sale and the time and energy of the newsboys is conserved. Seldom now that more than three thousand papers pass over the wholesale counter, and these are bought in good part by boys whose mart is nearer the home of THE NEWS than the center of the city.

In the days when white paper was cheap, little thought was given to the wasting of a thousand papers, as when extras arrived in the neighborhood of great factories after the men had ended their day's work. Then the final sport extras were held invariably until the end of the baseball games. But the prod-igal waste had to end, and today not only the early editions but the extras and the night edition "go to bed," as the shop parlance has it, promptly at their appointed minute.

Numerous other economies have been instituted in recent years which would seem, on the surface, to be picayunish, but which the present scale of newspaper production makes not merely advisable but necessary. Sisal twine, for example, is used to tie bundles of papers for shipment out of town. One and a half tons of this twine are consumed monthly, which, at the July, 1918, market price, cost $1,035. A year before, the bill would have been $825; two and a half years before, a little over $300. And at any price it is hard to get. Now, not only does THE NEWS have state agents return twine, but, wherever possible, it is dispensed with and leather straps substituted. These, though the initial cost is high, may be used indefinitely. Wrapping paper is saved, labeling becomes unnecessary, accounting is simplified, deliveries are obtained with greater speed, and the work of the truck driver and his "jumper" is greatly lessened by the employment of bulk instead of package delivery to agencies throughout the metropolitan district. Another item of which the layman might lose sight, is paste. The reduction in wrapping brought down the consumption, but THE NEWS still uses seven barrels a month.

The use of government mail bags in large numbers has led to the installation of holders such as are employed in the post offices, affixed to the under side of

There Is No Man-Handling of Huge Bundles of Paper in the Mailing Room.

Forty-One Automobiles Are Required to Distribute THE DETROIT NEWS.

the steel mailing room tables, where also are twine reels and disappearing paste pots. Daily the mailing room requires two hundred and fifty mail bags, but Sundays the bulk of the newspaper sends the number up to about five hundred.

Transportation charges for Sunday editions are not a matter to be sniffed at, for the total number of pages of one issue averages about fifteen million, and the weight runs close to a quarter of a million pounds. Of this, about one-fourth is delivered out of Detroit by mail, express, special electric car and automobile. Deliveries are made by automobile as far as thirty miles from the city. Two special electric trains have been employed at times over routes more than a hundred miles long, to carry the Sunday paper, though three special interurban cars now render adequate service.

Seven times a day editions are issued, each revised to include the latest news. The day of more numerous editions has passed, though time was when more than a dozen went forth from THE NEWS building. The heaviest "run" of today consists of 120,000 papers, struck off in an hour and thirty-five minutes; that is to say, in excess of 1,250 complete papers, regardless of size, every minute. To distribute these papers to the public through agents and street salesmen entails the maintenance of elaborate automotive equipment, consisting of thirty-seven trucks and four roadsters, one third electric, the rest gasoline; so it is quite to be expected that THE NEWS should maintain charging stations throughout the shipping room, and a repair shop capable of insuring efficient and continuous operation of the cars. They must stand severe punishment in the service of the reader.

The contrasting picture is drawn by a member of the staff who has been with THE NEWS from its birth. He had a single push cart with which to take papers to trains, a thousand or so in bundles, and he was allowed usually seven or eight minutes to reach the Michigan Central or the Brush Street depots. Sometimes they were hard pressed for time, and Mr. Scripps would signal with his fingers the number of blocks the boy must run and the number he could walk. If the load was extraordinary, or in winter if the snow was deep, the lad was assisted by newsboys, hired to tug on a rope attached to the front of the cart. Volunteer help was common enough, and indeed necessary, at a time when the whole staff of THE NEWS numbered about thirty.

The shipping room in the new building is a full block long, running from Fort Street to Lafayette Boulevard, so that one-way traffic is possible. Its width is fifty feet, allowing for easy manipulation of automobiles at the center of the room, where the loading platform is located, and near which trucks make delivery of the rolls of print paper or take away accumulating bales of waste. Bronze doors with glass windows, at either end of the room, reveal the condition of traffic in the street to the outgoing driver, and they are opened and closed automatically.

Here, in the heat of the day's work, sometimes may be seen the beginning and the end of the long story of newspaper production: the mountain of print paper coming on creaking wheels to Mahomet from the spruce forests of the north, telling no story but of mastery in woodcraft, chemistry and transportation; and, passing it, outward bound, other mountains, not white but gray with the glad and sad tidings of the deeds and the thoughts of men.